TWIN FLAME OR INSANE

Connecting With Your Divine Partner

CHAZETTEE MITCHELL

Passionate Intentions LLC
Jacksonville, FL

Twin Flame or Insane:
Connecting With Your Divine Partner

ISBN 978-0-578-98050-8

Copyright © 2021 by Chazettee Mitchell
Jacksonville, FL 32244

Published by Passionate Intentions LLC
6455 Argyle Forest Blvd
Jacksonville, FL 32244
www.passionateintentions.com

Printed in the United States of America. All rights reserved under International Copyright Law. Contents and/or cover may not be reproduced in whole or in part in any form without the express written consent of the Publisher.

This book is dedicated to my Twin Flame without whom none of this would have occurred, and there would be no story to tell.

No longer in the valley

Ase'

TABLE OF CONTENTS

• • •

Preface *1*
Introduction *5*

What is a Twin Flame 9
Believe in Magic 17
The Biggest Mistake 21
Who is He 25
The One 35
Any Means Necessary 43
Conclusion (Or So I Thought) 47
And Yet The Saga Continues 49
We Meet At Last 55

PREFACE

• ◉ •

I came across you inadvertently and dismissed you. You weren't my "normal type". I didn't see the possibilities at the time, but then you kept being presented to me until eventually I took the bait. I learned from you and then one day I was like "Hey there's something to this". Our connection strengthened and became like no other. I could feel you, all of your emotions. You could feel mine too.

Twin Flame Or Insane

I would be at work and get pissed off because something didn't go my way and you would text me a heart as if you knew that's what I needed in that moment. You did, but at the time I wasn't familiar with the concept of a twin flame. All I knew was this was something entirely different than anything I'd ever experienced... well I can't really say that exactly like that because before this encounter, I met my soulmate, or karmic, or false twin. Whatever you want to call it. He was the one that introduced me to the idea of having a person in this world that you are connected to like no other. He was my first so many things. He could read my thoughts. I could even demonstrate the phenomenon to others. I would say "watch, he's gonna call," and then the phone would ring. He wasn't shit though, just another narcissist, but the catalyst to my Twin Flame journey. As I started to research these topics I came to know that this was all a part of the process. You'll have a false twin to introduce you to the possibilities of the real one. Setting the stage sort of speak. As I dug further in for more knowledge I discovered how rare this thing really is, and that there are specific events that take place leading up to the REUNION. See twin flames are one in the same. One soul That splits into two bodies and then spends the rest of eternity trying to find its way back to itself. In my case, the male took on the majority of the feminie energy, while I exhibited more masculine energy in our dynamic. It is said that once the two unite, a transfer takes place and eventually everything balances out. Doesn't that sound beautiful? If only it were that simple.

Introduction

• • •

As I began my own twin flame journey, I became compelled to write this book. There is so much conflicting information on the topic that doing your own research can become very frustrating. We live in a time of information overload, and with the fact that EVERYONE, whether qualified or not, has access to some type of platform where they can spread whatever information they choose, whether it's actual fact or not. The journey to uniting with your twin flame is complicated enough as it is without adding the non factual opinions of others. With all things, always consider your source and their intentions. Are they coming from a place of unconditional love or bitterness? Experience is always our best teacher. Even so, we don't need to experience everything ourselves to gain this knowledge. We are able to learn through the experiences of others. Especially if you happen to be an empath, that is an added bonus. So it is with great pleasure that I share with you my journey down the path of twin flame union. This book is entitled "Twin Flame or Insane." I could answer the question right now when I tell you that "Absolutely yes," twin flames are real and "No, you're not insane," although at times you may think you are. Now that I've answered that for you I really could be finished here, right? Unless of course you are interested in learning more details of what to look for on your journey, how to know if you're even on the right path, or the difference between a twin flame, false twin, karmic partner, or soulmate. Maybe you would simply like to compare notes about what's going on in your own journey. All of that is up to you. I will assume that if you are reading this book the topic surely is of interest to you for some reason other than coincidence. In fact, it is a promising way to confirm that you are definitely on the path of twin flame union. Hopefully you'll find some gems to help soothe your wandering mind and provide you with peace, hope, patience, and joy as you embark upon one of the most beautiful experiences this life has to offer. The path to true love.

WHAT IS A TWIN FLAME

• • •

There are several terms used to describe relationships and partners that we experience during our lifetime. I would like to bring clarity to these terms, and define them properly so that we are able to make the proper distinction.

Karmic Partner: Enters your life to help you grow at a soul level, and clear karma between each other. This relationship usually ends once the lessons are learned.

We generally will have multiple karmic partners in our lifetimes, depending upon what lessons we need to learn.

Soulmate: A person with whom lies a natural affinity or deep connection. This relationship does not always have to be romantic. When we are in the company of our soulmate, we are at peace, and we can be our authentic selves and feel completely comfortable. Although soulmates can marry, they actually make the best friends.

Twin Flame: Your own soul shared across two physical beings. Both experience a constant yearning to reconnect. This relationship is all about speeding up your spiritual development, releasing wounds, removing blockages, and leading you to true self love. This relationship tends to be incredibly challenging.

With that being said, karmic partners make up the majority of our failed relationships. They were necessary for us to learn what we want from relationships by exposing us to what we don't want. They usually start off hot and heavy but eventually they take a turn for the worst and we leave these relationships with lessons learned and boundaries in place.

The soulmate is a deeper connection than a karmic partner. As I said before, these relationships don't always tend to be romantic. Think of the people in your life that you love the most. The ones you would fight for. These relationships provide so much comfort, as you can be exactly who you are without judgments. As with karmic partners, it is possible to have multiple soulmates over lifetimes.

Finally we have the twin flame. This relationship is truly the deepest connection you will ever have with another person. Like the karmic partner, you will learn from your twin flame, but the lessons aren't as hard. You will not be left with regret and doubt, but instead the lessons you learn from your twin flame will elevate you and make you stronger. Where your karmic partner teaches you lessons about relationships, your twin flame teaches you lessons about yourself, and they do it from a place of unconditional love. Of all the types of partners you will encounter, your twin flame relationship will be the most important, and it is the one that influences your soul's journey to ascension.

I would appreciate it if you would take a moment to reflect on your own situation. What is it about this person that makes you know in your heart that they are your twin flame? Use this page to write out the characteristics that would classify them as such. Do they have traits that align with any of the other possible types of partners? There are no right or wrong answers here, just some assistance with putting things into perspective.

_____

_____

_____

_____

_____

_____

Twin Flame Or Insane

Chazettee Mitchell

BELIEVE IN MAGIC

• • •

All people have a level of magic, whether they are aware of it or not. Once they tap into their spiritual nature they can utilize and strengthen their gifts. In the case of twin flames one of the pair is usually more spiritually advanced than the other. It was my counterpart who held most of the magic in my situation. Prior to embarking upon the twin flame journey, I believed in coincidence and chance; luck even. I had begun to realize that I could think of someone and they would call, but I attributed that to coincidence rather than channeling. I could want something so bad that it consumed most of my thoughts and then eventually it would somehow materialize in my life. I considered that chance or luck, but not manifestation. So yes, relationships are a very important part of self discovery. Some say that self discovery is the sole purpose of the relationship between twin flames, and that the pair don't always end up together. At this point, I'm unable to provide a definitive answer for that based upon my own experiences. My journey has not ended. If you were to search the internet for answers, you are guaranteed to be bombarded with both sides of the spectrum. There are those that describe their twin flame journey as the most beautiful experience of their life that ended with a happily-ever-after. Then there are those that will say it was the most painful, traumatizing, horrific thing they'd ever succumb to. Lastly, you have the majority of people that fall somewhere in the middle. They'll tell you they learned a lot and have an appreciation for the experience. You will get a plethora of responses, and they will leave you more confused than when you start your search. Not to mention, you should always consider your sources and their level of understanding. That can be nearly impossible to truly gauge on the internet. The lady whose blog says you should run for dear life at all costs probably was never dealing with her twin flame to begin with, but rather a narcissist. The best way for me to explain it is that when you know, you just know. The universe knows, your spirit guides know, and they will bring every synchronicity into your awareness to confirm it for you. You must be open and receptive to receive the information. This is when you'll start growing spiritually and unlocking your own gifts. Let your zest for love provide you the drive to become the best version of yourself. When you look at this way, you can't lose. In the beginning of my journey, I found myself constantly wondering and questioning whether or not this was the real thing. It consumed most of my thoughts. To be completely honest, there are still times when doubt creeps in. Those are merely indications of the work I still have left to do. I understand that we are one soul, and with that being the case, we never truly are apart.

THE BIGGEST MISTAKE

• • •

One of the biggest, if not the biggest, mistakes that you can make on your twin flame journey is trying to explain your thoughts, feelings, and emotions to a person that is not evolved enough to understand the process. It will lead you to be discouraged, and to experience great frustration. The fact that it's nearly impossible to find a person who will understand your experiences, or who can listen at best, will make you feel lonely, misunderstood, and nearly insane. Others will try to guide you with their logic, but the most important thing to understand here is that logic has very little to do with it. The main lesson in all of this is about trusting your own instincts, and listening to your own voice. Your higher self does not adhere to the mundane standards of this world. The twin flame journey is the ultimate spiritual journey, and it is a very personal thing. Not many will be able to relate to you. There will even be times when you have experiences that are so foreign to you, that you can not find the words to verbalize the situation. This is where confusion can come in, and you start to feel lonely. The spiritual path is in fact a lonely path. You will let go of so many people and relationships along the way. It is heart wrenching, but necessary. It is the only way to evolve into your highest self.

Who is He

• • •

My twin flame entered my awareness sometime in 2018. I was sent a video through social media of a man giving his opinion on a random topic. I was like "OK...and". I personally, can be a bit antisocial, even on social media. Go figure. I often am annoyed by receiving unsolicited shares, and group invites. This situation was no different. Whatever his topic of conversation was, I was unimpressed and uninterested.

Even so, this was the moment that this man's existence even became known to me. Months had gone by and I hadn't given this man a second thought. Then one day me and another woman were having a conversation about feminine hygiene of all things. This happens to be the same woman who loves sending me videos on social media. We were discussing the controversy of to douche or not to douche, that was the question. We delved into how modern society insists that the vagina is self cleansing and requires no help, and we both agreed that that concept was bullshit. Later that very same evening, this woman tagged me in a video on social media where a man was addressing this very topic. Now what are the chances of that. Not to mention, it was the same man from the previous videos. To be honest, I was annoyed by being tagged in a video explaining the proper way to clean my vagina. Also the fact that the message was being delivered by a man was kind of off putting, with his homely looking ass. I will admit, however, that I did watch some of the video, and he did in fact bring up some things that I had never considered. I remember when I was a little girl and my grandmother always kept that red bag hanging up in the shower. As a kid I had no idea what it was, and unfortunately in my family no one ever talked about subjects like that. According to this man on the internet, this is what women should be using rather than the feminine products that are marketed to us. He also attributed the decreased use of the douche bag to the increase of feminine hygiene issues, disease, and infection. What he said actually made a lot of sense to me. As a result, I went searching at several drug stores, but eventually I ended up ordering my own douche bag online. Again he was dismissed. Fast forward to December 2018. I experienced a tremendous loss from the death of my fifteen year old son. He chose to take the road of suicide as a means to an end of his pain on earth. As to be expected I was devastated. Guess what happened. The same woman reached out yet again with a video from this same man. As I'm reflecting on this, it almost seems unreal. The irony of his topic. Suicide of all things. He spoke about how our children are not really ours, and lots of other hermetic concepts that were foreign to me at the time. I listened, and all in all his video brought a sense of peace. I actually tried to share the video to my social media account, but if you can, recount the day in 2018 when social media crashed.

It was also the day when people who had specific cell phone providers were unable to make or receive calls. Yes, this was THAT day. So once again I had been given some jewels and this man was dismissed. Keep in mind, at this time, I hadn't really paid much attention to his name, and my only access to his videos had been from this woman that continuously shared and forwarded his messages to me. Fast forward nearly two years later. The same woman sent me another video on social media. At this time I was in a completely different head space. The death of my son affected me in so many ways, and I had begun to take my journey down the path of spirituality much more seriously. I had always been interested in such topics, but more so as an observer, or an outsider looking in. At this point it was becoming more of a way of life for me.

It happens this way for most people. If you aren't born into a life of spiritual practice, it takes some traumatic event to occur in your life that makes you start to question everything. So nonetheless, I watched the video. I can't remember the exact topic but whatever it was was enough to resonate with me to the point where I started watching his videos regularly. Eventually I sent out a friendly request, which he accepted. I was kind of surprised because I noticed he didn't have many friends at the time. As I mentioned, I was not heavily into social media, and things that were trendy were normally the things I avoided. This man was definitely not trendy. He had his own way of expressing himself, and his ideals were not mainstream. I also noticed that the videos he posted to his account didn't have many viewers. This worked for me. At some point he uploaded a video that made me reach out to him. This was something that is very out of character for me, but it felt right at that moment. I was deeply moved by his topic of discussion, and I felt he should know that even though he didn't have tons of viewers his video had made a difference to someone. I was completely shocked to get a response back. It was truly unexpected. As time went on, I continued to learn from this man. Whenever he posted something I appreciated I didn't hesitate to let him know, and he was always very receptive. By this time I was working the midnight shift in a hospital. I had a super easy job with a lot of downtime. I started to fill this time by watching his videos, and learning new things. Eventually I came across a video that would alter my entire world from that day forward. Most of my life, I had considered myself to be a unique individual. I was always able to mingle with any crowd, but I never truly felt a sense of belonging anywhere. Over time I learned to accept that about myself, and simply navigated the world as a loner at heart. In this particular video, he described his ideal woman and the type of relationship they would have. He was very descriptive in describing everything from her physical attributes to the sound of her voice. He had given an in depth description of me. So here I was feeling as if I am an outcast, and that my qualities somehow made me different from all of the others. Yet this man was reading me like a book. It made me question everything I had thought was unique to me. Was I, in fact, a "type"? I noticed that this video had been uploaded back in 2018, well before he even knew I existed. It sent chills through my body and it made me want to know more about this man because up until this point I had not dug any deeper into who he actually was. I had yet to discover his many dimensions. I didn't know that he made products because at this point he was not advertising them. It was at this juncture that I began to take a serious interest in finding out more about who this man was.

The One

• • •

I started to look at him with a completely different set of eyes. Oftentimes it seemed as if he were speaking directly into my soul. The sensation was strange, but a good strange. A comfortable stranger. I felt as if he understood me, and that was refreshing in and of itself because I never really believed anyone else ever did. The more I gave my attention to this man, the stranger things became. It was nothing short of magical to be completely honest. The synchronicities, vivid thoughts, and daydreams. Eventually it became too much to be mere coincidence. Something supernatural was occurring here. I reached out to him in a completely different context. He told me he felt the same types of feelings, and that it was a rare occurrence for him because he is very guarded. He did mention that he was not looking for a partner. "Undateable" was how he described it. I started to notice his following was much greater than I had previously realized, and I explained to him that I didn't want to be looked at as just another of his groupies. These were the words that we spoke to each other, but the attraction didn't end there. It actually grew stronger. It was as if our minds and emotions communicated with each other in another dimension that didn't require our consent. As I started to feel myself become more and more attached, I started to get concerned and I felt the need to protect my heart. Even though he expressed that he didn't want anything more than a friendship, everything else revealed the opposite. Then one day I noticed he uploaded a video to a social media site. The video was not his best work. It was terrible actually, and that was very unlike him. Normally he spoke with great confidence and was always self assured. This video was certainly off. The more I analyzed it, the more I realized he sounded like me. I've never been very outspoken until something upsets me, and public speaking even in high school, made me cringe. As I watched his video, I realized that he was picking up my mannerisms. This is when I decided to back off. I saw him as a man who had great potential to teach the world, and I felt that I shouldn't get in the way of that. I considered him to be out of my league, and I vowed to step way back. I stopped reaching out to him and even stopped watching his videos. I simply put my focus in other directions. For two, or maybe three months I continued on with no contact. Then on July 15th (I remember the exact date) something came over me. I wanted to check in on him, and see what was new so I went to his social media account. His most current status was "Bae I miss you" with a photo of himself. I was overcome with emotion. It was as if he had summoned me back to him. After that things just became more and more magical. Extremely too many things for me to include every detail, but it was enough to make me feel that this man was "The One", and that the answer was not to dismiss him from my life, but to elevate myself to meet him at his level. He would be the one to help me heal. I needed to somehow get close to him to explore this further. Once I made this realization, it seemed as if he started to back away from me. We undoubtedly took turns with the runner chaser dynamic. Whenever it was my turn to be the chaser, my ego would step in and I would say "I'm done with this", and try to put him behind me. Every time I would call myself ending the situation, he would be brought back to me in the most random ways. There was no escaping this. Whenever I would spend time meditating or speaking at the altar with my ancestors asking for a life partner, and an end to my loneliness, all signs pointed to this man. EVERY SINGLE TIME. He has even shown up in tarot readings that I've done for myself, and ones that I have had done by others. Then one day, with no prior announcement, he let me know that he was in my state, and that he wanted to see me. This could not have been more of an inopportune time for me. It was the day before I was scheduled to start a new job. Not only that, but he was a five hour drive away from me. It just was not feasible at that time. There were many times after that where I looked back and wished I went to meet with him. The start date of the job could have been rescheduled. I do understand now why it didn't happen. I apologetically told him that I would come to his state the following month to celebrate my birthday. He was cool with it. I booked all of the reservations for the trip, and at the very last moment, my car broke down. To be honest, I could have still taken the trip because all of my accommodations were already paid for, but something just didn't feel right about taking the trip at that time so I canceled everything. At this point I think we both were extremely frustrated. It just seemed like we weren't supposed to ever meet up. The meeting was supposed to have already occurred several times, and every time something stood in the way. I didn't want him to think that I was some weird sort of "catfish" situation, so I let him know that rather than tell him I'm coming to see him and then later having to tell him all bets are off, my next plan of action would be to pop up in his state like he did mine, and to call him once I was actually there. He had kind of a "yeah whatever" type of attitude When I expressed this to him. Months went by until finally I couldn't take it anymore. I was ready to be with my man by any means. Let me tell you how that turned out…

ANY MEANS NECESSARY

• ● •

I decided enough was enough I could not go on longing for his presence. I decided that this was it. Nothing would stop me this time. It is funny now to look back at how clueless I was about divine timing, and how little control we have over it. I planned my trip a month in advance without his knowledge. I put in a request for the days off with my job, booked my flight, and took care of all the other arrangements. As the date came closer I noticed my job had not approved my request for time off. I'm pretty sure it had something to do with it being the holiday season. I simply resubmitted the request without giving it a second thought. I made arrangements for someone to drop me off at the airport. All plans were in place. The day had finally arrived. I'm pretty sure I didn't get much sleep the night before because of all the excitement. I reorganized my suitcase for about the third time. I was so nervous I decided I'd have a glass of wine to help myself calm down. Then another, and another. I started to feel myself getting tired. I had about four hours before I needed to leave for the airport. I decided to lay down. Do I even need to tell you what happened next? When I woke up from the wine induced slumber, my flight had left an hour prior. I had about five missed calls from my driver, and an email from the airline. I was so upset. I called my brother to share my dilemma. His response was that it sounded like it was not meant to happen, and that maybe I should reconsider. I refused his advice. I told him the only way I wasn't going was if the plane didn't go. I paid an additional fee to catch the next flight which was scheduled to leave at 6:38 the next morning. I remember calling my driver at around 6:00 p.m. and asking him to take me to the airport right then. He thought I was insane to wait at the airport for twelve hours, and he may have had valid concerns, but I was not about to let anything else go wrong. My mind was made up. Twelve hours later, I got on the plane. There was a short layover in another city. It didn't bother me at all. When the time came, I boarded my final flight. For once in my life I was able to have patience. Then the most beautiful thing occurred. The wheels landed on the runway in his city at exactly 11:11 a.m. What greater confirmation could I receive that I was on the correct path. The pilot proceeded to welcome us and update us with local information. He then announced it was safe to take our phones off of airplane mode. It was at that moment the time on my phone went back an hour to adjust to the different time zone. Needless to say, the trip was a disaster. I did not get to see him, and once I returned home I ended up losing my job. This was surely a message from the universe that yes he is the one, but that I could not skip out on doing the inner work first. I was too early.

Conclusion
(Or So I Thought)

• • •

I've been writing this book as I go through these experiences. Each chapter was created as each moment unfolded. Now, I find myself at the end of the story. Unfortunately, I'm unable to say that this is the part where I get to look my twin flame in his eyes and we share a sacred kiss. To be completely honest, I never even got the opportunity to look into his eyes; to experience what I've heard described as "soul shock". I asked myself how could I be sure he was even the one after all this time? I believe that the main objective of the twin flame is to put you in your place spiritually. They open your eyes to new images, dreams, and possibilities. You look at life differently, and with profound purpose. Although you are never guaranteed to unite in this realm, this person will remain in your heart and in your memories for the rest of eternity. Some days will be harder than others, but one thing is for certain. You will never be able to go back to being the person you were before you came into the awareness of your twin flame. And that is how you can be assured they are the one.

And Yet The Saga Continues

• ◉ •

I had reached a point of great frustration on my journey of twin flame union. I'd made several attempts to bring us together and failed each time. My counterpart was an avid runner, so that made things very difficult. I could no longer stomach the rejection, and I had found myself exhausted and defeated. I was tired of being consumed by this obsession, and I knew I needed to let go. I actually started seeking out other males to entertain, with no genuine attraction. I was merely trying to divert my attention. Then in the blink of an eye everything changed. I'll give you the simplistic version of events because otherwise you may end up having questions that I'm not prepared to answer, at least not in this book. I walked around in a slump continuously. I tried pulling myself together but my attitude reflected my dismay. The people closest to me felt it the most. So much so that I was confronted and told I needed to go see him. I was surprised to hear this, and kind of annoyed at the same time. I had been trying so hard to forget him. Rather than explaining this, I was more interested in learning why I was being told I needed to go see him. The response I received was that it was obvious that I was in love. "You need to figure this thing out", was exactly how it was expressed to me, and it was suggested that I go that week. I wanted to object, and continue sticking with my decision to let it go, but to hear someone explain to me how they could see my suffering was enough to influence me to relight the flame and try again. After all, when you really want something already, it doesn't take much persuasion. To be honest, I don't think I'll ever give up on love, no matter how many times I've been deceived and hurt. I immediately started looking for flights. The most affordable one was scheduled to leave the very next morning. I started to get that uneasy feeling in my stomach. My head filled with doubts. What if I was wasting my time and money yet again. Do I call him now and tell him I'm coming, or do I call him once I reach his city? So many decisions to make in so little time. I decided this was it. I wasn't going to call and give him an opportunity to refuse. The next morning, I was on that flight. Once I landed, I checked myself into a hotel room. I was beside myself. I decided that this time would be different. Rather than focus my entire trip on meeting up with this man, I decided I would find activities in the area to occupy my time. It was either that, or show up at his door unannounced, prepared for whatever reaction I'd receive. I decided on the latter. I spent several hours composing myself before finally reaching out. I elected to text him a simple "hello", to which I received almost an immediate response. There was an exchange of small talk until finally I invited him out for a drink. It was at that point that I let him know I was in his area. His texting became delayed. He eventually blew me off with an excuse of feeling ill from being out the night before. I didn't press the issue, but I was let down once again. I felt so foolish. What kind of fucking game was this. My foolishness began to turn to anger. I started to reconsider the thought of popping up at his place, and although I knew nothing good could become of that, I needed something to put an end to the longing in my heart. Perhaps uncovering the fact that he was married and very much in love with another woman could be the medicine I needed, and yet once again I selected the high road. Instead, I came to the conclusion that I may as well have fun whilst I was there. I spent the first day of my trip exploring the city. I actually took a walking tour where I was familiarized with some of the history of the area. I checked out an antique bookstore, and I also pleased my palate with the city's famous cuisine. Later that evening, once I had returned to my hotel room, I sent a text to see if he felt any better. He didn't respond. I went to bed. The next day I texted him again and once again nothing. I text him one final time saying something like "you're really gonna do this", and then he called. He explained that he was working and extremely busy, and that he wasn't trying to avoid me. I called bullshit, but how could I argue with a man that had no idea I was flying into town to see him. He pacified me by agreeing to meet with me on the following day. That also happened to be the day of my departing flight.

WE MEET AT LAST

• • •

I woke up on the final day of my trip with extreme excitement. I was finally going to get to be face-to-face with the man who had stolen my heart from afar. My nerves had kicked in like never before. I spent the morning poolside trying to calm myself down before check out time. Finally the moment arrived. Once again there was a letdown. Initially the plan was that he would take an extended lunch to meet with me. When we spoke, he explained that would not be possible, and that he could only step away for a short amount of time. I agreed because at this point there was nothing left to lose. I could walk away from this experience with clarity and closure from a logical perspective. It seemed to me that his interest was simply not there. Every reason that he had for avoiding me demonstrated that. My heart had an entirely different outlook. It could be argued that I was inconsiderate to assume he could drop everything to meet up with me with no prior notice. At this moment I felt like a full blown obsessed stalker, but then not really. What kept me from going completely over the edge into that category was the fact that he had been communicating back-and-forth with me this entire time. We shared intimate discussions, and personal images. The more

I sat and reflected on everything, the more confused I became. The terms gaslighting and breadcrumbing even came to mind. Then my phone rang. He had arrived at my location and was trying to pinpoint my exact whereabouts. My heart started to flutter. This was the moment that had become the most important in my life. I gave him a description of the car I was driving and where I was parked. He said he had spotted me. I looked around searching for my missing link. I didn't see him anywhere. I stepped out of the car to extend my field of view and finally I found him. He was slowly approaching me. I damn near passed out. I remember being overcome by a sudden feeling of disassociation. It was as if my soul had completely left my body and I was watching the event unfold. I honestly can't even remember what our first words were to each other. That's how out of sorts I was. It could have been the combination of my nerves and the vodka I had recently finished. We spent a total of about fifteen minutes in each other's presence. I was finally able to wrap my arms around him in an embrace, and to experience his scent. Roughly fifteen minutes later, he was gone. Was it everything that I had fantasized it would be? Absolutely not. There were no fireworks, no feeling as if I was suddenly complete. We never even exchanged our first kiss. I left with a few pictures of us together and even more confusion and longing for him than I had before we met.

www.ingramcontent.com/pod-product-compliance
Lightning Source LLC
Chambersburg PA
CBHW032017290426
44109CB00013B/699